Christmas MIRACLE —on— 19TH STREET

Jeanie Breedwell

Copyright © 2020 by Jeanie Breedwell.

ISBN   Softcover   978-1-951469-71-9

All rights reserved. No part of this book may be reproduced or transmitted in any form or by any means, electronic or mechanical, including photocopying, recording, or by any information storage and retrieval system without express written permission from the author, except in the case of brief quotations embodied in critical reviews and certain other non-commercial uses permitted by copyright law.

Printed in the United States of America.

To order additional copies of this book, contact:
Bookwhip
1-855-339-3589
https://www.bookwhip.com

The little girl's name was Tammy. She lived with her mother and father. Her parents didn't have jobs and they were really poor.

Tammy was so sad, her mother and father told her that they are not celebrating Christmas this year. "What do I do?" Tammy asked. She knows that there are children like her who won't be able to celebrate Christmas as well. "I have got to talk to mother." She said. "We need to pray for a miracle."

"On 19th streets what are you saying?" asked her mother. "We need to pray for our town,

God can change things. Don't God answer prayers?" asked her mother. "Yes, he does he loves me, he died for everyone." said Tammy. "Then, He will listen to us when we pray, I am sure He will." said her mother. "I have faith, don't you mother?" asked Tammy. "Where are you going with this? I believe in God, He will send a miracle to our little neighborhood." said her mother.

Tammy asked her mother if she can go to their playhouse. "My friends are there waiting" said Tammy. "Check in later I need to know where you are." said her mother. "I will let you know later I want to talk to my friends about what we need to do." Tammy replied. On her way to where her friends are she was thinking about what to say. It is 18 days till Christmas.

She saw sad faces when she got there. "What was wrong?" she asked. Tammy thought to herself, maybe they got the same news she had about no Christmas. Tammy told the girls that they have to do something and they agreed.

One of the girls asked "What do you have in mind?" "We need to pray" Tammy replied. "Do you all believe in Jesus?" They all drop their heads. She could see something was wrong and that they need to pray to Jesus, they need that miracle in their neighborhood.

"I need to go home I promised mother I would check in. I will be back later." Tammy told her friends. When Tammy made it home "Mother, I am here." "Okay dear." "I need to go I will be back, I have 17 girls waiting for me to return. I will be back." said Tammy. She hugged her mother and left.

Tammy met with the girls. They sat on the ground and talked about praying. "We need to ask Jesus for a Miracle on our street." Tammy said to the girls. I do not have my Bible it's at home I will bring it tomorrow. We will meet here again at 10:00 AM tomorrow, I will be reading about Jesus' birth, Matthew and Mark and more. It's from Gods holy word we need to come up with a name for us.

"I was thinking about the 18 Musketeers." "That sounds good." said one of the girls. "Yes!" said Betty. "Like the show, Mickey Mouse." "Now that we have a name for the group I need to go home mother will be worried." said Tammy. The girls said goodbye to each other. When Tammy made it home, she was ready for bed she was so tired. Her mother was waiting for her. "Mother I am going to bed I will see you in the morning." She kisses her mother goodnight.

When she got to her room, she fell down on her knees and prayed. "Dear Jesus I know you answer prayers and nothing is too big for you, we need a miracle on our street. Not for me just my friends and family if that's ok."

She went to the window, sat down looking at so many stars in the sky and the big moon, God's creation. It's time to go to sleep.

The next morning she got dressed and started thinking, tears ran down her cheeks as she remembered her brother. On his death if it was on the news, why didn't someone say something? She did not understand? Tammy did not tell her mother that she found out about it. It is time she talks to her mother about Billy, her brother. Why didn't her grandmother tell her it was a closed nobody talk about it?

She went into the kitchen. Her mother was setting at the old broken down table. "Good morning mother." Tammy greeted her mother. "When I get older I will marry a rich man and buy you whatever you want." Tammy said. "Honey that will be sometime you just stays your little self and do what God wants and you will be fine I know you would do anything for me thank you anyway." Her mother replied.

"You sound like me, we were poor. Yes, my Daddy worked but it took what he made to keep us food and clothes." Her mother said.

"I am sorry mother I did not know." Tammy replied. "It's ok dear God keep us feed and clothes for us to wear. I had brothers that eat you out of a house and home." her mother replied.

"We fight the entire time." "Mother speaking of your brother what happened to my brother Billy? Found the newspaper. It would have been nice to have a little brother." "Honey you are younger than he was." "I am?" "Yes, you are."

"Can you fill me in, what happened?" "When he was two years old, he got into some poison. Before I got to him he was gone."

"Your daddy and I cried for months. Your daddy remembers him coming to our room before he went to bed kissing us goodnight.

He did that every night, but mother he was a big boy. Why would he do that?" Her mother wanted to stop talking about her brother.

"Oh yes, your father had the name for your brother Billy boy." Tammy did not want to let go she wanted to know more. "In the paper, he had a blue shirt on he was so pretty. I was in the kitchen cooking when I hear him coughing."

"I can still hear your daddy calling him I feel like it was my fault; did you read the paper no I was surprised when I saw it." "Mother you never said anything about your family. You want me to tell you about my family?"

"My mother come from Georgia your grandpa come from Chicago he came down to Georgia that is where he met my mother."

"She was working at a fast food place. He stops to get hamburger and fries, my mother waiting on him."

"They started talking he was on his way back to Chicago. After he met my mother he got a motel and him and mother started seeing each other for a while then one day he got a call from his mother he had to go to war. He went where mother work he told her the sad news that upset my mother so much he did not know how long before."

"He would see her again, her name is Brenda his name is Bob. He was in the war so long but she wrote him and he wrote."

"One day she got a call, he was missing. This upset her then she got a knock at her door. Two soldiers, they gave her the bad news his parents told them where she lived the mother said he was so happy since he met my mother."

"My mother said, No lord I just met him do not take him from me. My mother said she could not eat nor sleep. It upset my grandmother she did not know what to do she tried to get her to eat she would not she just acted like she did not want to live; what happen mother will some months later my mother went shopping for your grandmother her friend went with her."

"When she returns home her mother met her at the door, she told her she had a surprise for her she told her to close her eyes; you have them close my mother said yes my Daddy reach out and put his arms around her she was so happy; he told her what happen he lost his dog tag."

"That is when they thought he was missing someone gave him another tag it belongs to a person that was dead that is when he came up killed but when he found out what happen it was taken care of, and he got to come home; there is some good news took care of the wedding that is it said Tammy yes am here yes mother you are; I was the first to be born 5 kids that was a good story yes I have wanted to tell you that so long." "Now I have got to get to the playhouse mother." She left she grab her Bible on her way out. As she got close to her friends she looks in her bag for her Bible.

When she made it to her friends she said, "I guess you are ready to listen to God's word? Did you all pray?" "Yes!" they all said. "I will read from Matt and Mark and more, Jesus was born in a manger on Christmas day his mother Mary gave birth to him. The wise men came to give him gifts and worship him, King Jesus."

"He died for us all does anyone have a Bible?" She could tell no one had a Bible this brought tears to her eyes it is getting late I have got to go home she hugs them and said, "See you all at ten in the morning." she left the way she came.

When she made it home her mother was worried, "Why are you late? You had me scared." "I was reading the word of God in my Bible" her Dad spoke, "Is it ok to read to your friends what about their parents?" "It's okay Dad now if it's okay. I need to go to my room. It's time for me to pray. "It's okay." said her Dad. She got down on her knees. "Dear Jesus it's me again I need you to help my friends and my mother and Daddy needs a job I do now want anything, but please help my friends they have nothing it could put a smile on their faces Jesus, I have got to go. Amen."

She went to the window, "Jesus I know you have been here I saw the 18 on all our houses she look at all the stars in the sky and the big moon all Gods creations."

The next morning she went to the kitchen where her mother was. "I am going to our playhouse." Are you? Oh dear." "Yes we named our group musketeers what do you think? We have a name for our group." "I think that is good." said her mother. "I have got to go they will be waiting for me."

On her way she meets this man asked her how she was doing. The man said, "Oh I know you, my daughter told me you read the Bible to her and some more girls." Tammy drops her head. what have I gotten my self into; the man said its ok my mother tried to teach me the Bible I would not listen; its ok to teach her if you want to; what is your daughter name its Betty 'yes I know her she told me you all come up with a name for the girls; yes we did you are so young I am nine years old that is so young yes you help us out when you took control; if you have faith it can happen now I need to go nicely talking to you just keep on doing what you have been doing; when she got to her friends you are late said one of her friends; Betty I just saw your Dad; I want to talk to; the Musketeers about the Bible afterward we will play; we all know Jesus died for us all; what was she saying the look on there faces he perform many miracles; listen he feed five thousand women men children, and there were 12 baskets left over that got there attention; that is why I need for you all to have faith in God; and pray for us all I saw the 18 in all our houses; so you believe in Jesus yes we do; we are happy now that you said you saw it too; it's getting late I need to go home; wait said one of the Girls can we pray for my dad; he dranks all the time and keeps my brother and me upset; when he comes home mother fights it is getting so bad; do you thank he will answer my prays; that is so sad; sure God will answer your prayers; they are fussing so much he dranks beer all at once it was like a dam burst open; one of them said her brother was living with a woman she was older than him was giving him drugs his mother; tried to get him to leave but .many more stores; I will pray for you; all nothing is too big for God; this is bigger than I thought she hug the girls and left; one of the girls said her mother drank she stays out all night sometimes her dad tried to help she did not want help; she was thinking about it on her way home; when she got there; her mother was waiting I need to talk to you' I listen what do you need? my friends are in trouble I need you to pray for them ok dear; tell me, child; what is going on my friends are having trouble at home; pray ok mother I will here is your peace of' of bread; thanks mother; Tammy began to think what it would look like to see new things in her house; she could see things that were not there; a new stove a new table for her mother; a freezer for food; tablecloth on her mother new table nice dishes to eat out of; food on the table chicken ham all different; vegetables and side dishes rugs on the floor; lights burning; her mind went into the bedroom a nice bed in her.

Room and dresser for her things to put some clothes in nice shoes in a closet where her clothes hung; Went to her mother room saw nice things for her mother and Daddy look outside saw anew car in the driveway; Tv in her room she looked back at her room saw some more nice things; everything was different as she could see; her mother saw her asleep weak up dear mother, I am not asleep; she went to her room as soon as she did' her knees hit the floor Jesus, I need you so bad to help my friends they are in trouble. I do not need; to tell you what goes on in our little Neighboorhood so sad just learn about it today, and lord do please; do not forget the miracle on 18 street; Amen; she went to the window to see the stares the moon God; creations 'she looked at her gown laying on her bed it brought back memories when her grandmother gave it to her; she was packing for her trip; she came across the gown here you can have this it was your cousin; she went with me on a trip I guess she left it in my it is your now what was her name? she was one of your aunt Ruth and uncle Toms daughters it ok she is; too big for it now thank you grandmother; patty was her name; she put her gown on and went to bed; the night went by fast the next morning Tammy went into her kitchen; her mother was not there she look of the window; saw the person live next door; she walked outside; ha my name is Terry my husband Tommy; died last year; what is your name; my name is Tammy I lived here for many years; I do not know why your family does not talk to me; here is you a drink; thank you, nice to meet you; now I was thinking when your family going to tell you about your; brother; my mother. she said he ate some poison; that is not true; did you read the paper no I just found; it; will you cousin was staying with your family he had a gun in his things he shot your brother; how do you know that? there was a trial it went on for a long time; your cushion was charged with murder' why did my mother tell me that story; I do not know read the paper; she went inside Tammy went back; in her house; her mother was at the table; I prayed for your group thank you mother; she grabs her Doll her mother said are you taken your doll? yes mother after I read my Bible we will play; when she got to her friends she saw a smile on there; facet they were saying since Jesus put the 18 on their houses he could answer there prays; we need to sit down so I can read the Bible; Jesus had many people to follow him he met the women at; the well he told her the water she drinks she would thirst; but the water he gives her she would never thirsty again it was like a fountain that keeps on going bubbly up running forever.'

John Baptized the father was so proud of Jesus now I am putting the Bible away we can play for; awhile; do anyone of you has a doll? she could see that they did not have a toy Tammy said that ok; Christmas is soon you can play with my dolls; take turns; God is so good; now I will see you tomorrow; when she got home her mother was the kitchen; where is your Doll she drops her head I wonder will she punished me if I tell her; she was scared her mother looked at her its ok come here I am not mad at you; I know you will bring your Doll home when you get ready; yes mother let me explain; my friends have no toys I let them keep my doll until Christmas they are passing it around; I will get it back; after Christmas; come here that is so good for you to share what you have with your friends; yes mother; God would like that; they are my little musketeers I am so proud of you; I felt sorry for them; here is you some gravy with your bread. mother I like the gravy I know you do thank you mother; after she got finished eating she was ready for bed; mother that was so good now may I go to my room?

When Tammy was in her room she could not wait to pry to God about her friends the family and miracle; on 18 street 'she went to sleep; the next morning; she went to the kitchen as before; her mother; was seating at the broken down table good morning mother; are you meeting with your little group? yes, mother reading from the holy word; I need to go if you need mei will be at our playhouse; I will be there for some time; ok dear so she left; on her way she was thinking of what to read about when Tammy got into her room; she could not wait she wainted to pray to reach God about her friends; The family and miracle on 18 street; she went to sleep; the next morning she went to the kitchen as before; Her mother was seated at the old broken down table; good morning mother good morning her mother said. Are you meeting with your little group? yes, mother reading from; The holy book.

I need to go you will know where I am at; if you need me; I will be there for some time; ok dear so she left; on her way; She was thinking on what to read about; I just want to tell them what Jesus means to me; The girls were ready; when she got there; lets all seat down; I wont to tell; You what Jesus is to me; first of all he know me before I was born; and he gave his life for me; he saved me we are a shell nothing in it' without Jesus; Tammy had there for a while;she look around her other people come to hear her; preached; Jesus fasted forty days and nights he prayed to the father; This was before he was hung on the cross; he asked the father to removed the cup from him; the father his well be done.

Jesus loves us so much; I ned to know is there anyone here that does not know the Father; I will lead you to him; just step foward Jesus is coming soon; you do not want to be left behind.

Tammy said lord we have lots here that wont to know you; dear love ones repeat after me; dear Jesus I ama sinner; please come into my heart; I will confess you to the world make a place in heaven for me Amen; lots of people accept Jesus that day; Tammy was so happy she saw Betty dad there; he come to her thank you so much; that is what I need 'all of the girls; Gave they hearts to Jesus.

Jesus is answer my prays before Christmas; most of the girls parents were there; that come foward; she was thanking Jesus; For saving the people in her neighborhood all of them were thankful to God for saving them; Tammy was talking to them; she said now we have more to pray with us; For Meracle here on this street; they all agree; it was like a great thing for her to carry out in her on words; now it was geting late; she looked; at

Her friends they all had tears in there eyes; She know they had accepted the Lord Jesus Christ; she went to them Iwill pray for all of you; yes they all said; she hug all; her friends; told them she would be back the next day.

When she was walking home; she noticed the ones gave the hearts to God; they wave at her with a big smile on there face; That made her feel good; when she got home her mother and Dad were there; she begain to tell them what happen; her mother was so proud of her; she asked her dad could you help me; what do you need kitten; that was the name he gave her when she was small; she like kittens; dad Iam starting a Revival at our playhouse; Could you put a sign up for me; On the post sure kitten I can; I will go there now; Tammy had made a diffrents in that neighborhood on 18stret she love the lord; she saw what he could do; he had saved around 50 people at her teaching; now most of; the people will come to her Revival; she was just geting started; she was looking for things to change; the devil had to go; this little girl was only 9 years old she wanted to feed them the word of God; her mother taught her what God could do.'

Now she was going to put the words into pratice; tell everyone about Jesus; what he could do for anyone; her dad is back; it is up kitten; thank you dad come here to your dad she went to her dad; I am so proud of you; you are so young but dad they need to know about Jesus; while I was there; people were watching me put up your sign; they were telling me about you; how you lead them to the lord; somethings else; you are famous; someone call the tv station you are going to be on the news; really dad? yes dear now tomorrow your mother and me will be there; to give you support; are you kidding dad? no I am not kidding; the word is out.'

Tammy was so happy; but dad mother I will be Nervous; you will be fine kitten said her dad; we will be there to cheer you on; You are doing this for Jesus; he is the one we wont people to know about; now it is time for bed said her mother; you have a big day ahead of you; yes mother goodnight mother and dad; they both said goodnight; in her room she got dress ready to pray.

Dear Jesus I want to be the best for you tomorrow; lead the sinners to repents; so they can live for you; help me lord I will be on nation tv lots of people will see me; I know with you there to help me I will make it Amen; she went to the window to look out she saw the stars and the wonderful moon God creations; then she went to bed; it was hard; For her to go to asleep.

When she did it was morning time to get up her dad said; big day for you; we will be going with you; so get the sleepness; out of you eyes; Lets go they are there already I guess; when they got there like; her dad said lots of people were there with channel 8 news; this is the sign I put up for you; looks good dad; thank you the speach begains; my name is Tammy I started out with my little group; telling them about Jesus; we talking about other things; most of the people know this is a poor neighborhood; we have nothing before I go any fether I wont to welcome all of you; people to my Revival; we meet here every day at 10 am; I feel like God wanted me to do this; I lead 50 people to Jesus yesterday; most of them live here channel 8 news we welcome you to our Revival; lets give channel 8 a welcome they all clamp; when it was all over the news people wanted to talk to Tammy; miss we are so glad to know you; your name is Tammy you are only 9 years old; yes I am; what made you want to do this? will I know that the friends here did not know Jesus we are all poor I was praying for miracle on our street; that is how it begain; that is something for a girl so young; wow she is something else; Tony and Sue they were talking between them self' that is right said Frank Smath out of Georgia you have a good day Tammy thank you; thanks for having me said Frank Smith we are sign off this is Frank Smith out of Georgia; Tammy begain to talk to her friends; they were so glad that Tammy was on the tv; her mother and dad were waiting on her; it was time to go home; she had lead more to Jesus; she was now realy famous; but it was not her; she said she give Jesus the credit he was the one saved all them people; she lead them to Jesus that is all; not her God is her leader her lord and savor she gives him all the credit she may be young God gave her wisdom' to help her make it though this world living in a world of trouble and Deceite and proverty Tammy wants to make diffrents in her little town and God is the answer; she is looking for; 'she has taken her first step; toward changing the out cast of the Neighborhood; to make it better; so the next creation would have a better place to live; She wants God in everything School jobs government; as she is growing older she plains to talk to anyone that will listen; she has got a touch on what she wants to do; make her State strong and Liberated so no one feel like they are in a valley; instead of on top of a mountain; Tammy was geting things together; to contined her preaching Gods world; now it was time for her to rest; she had some things; to tell God she need guidness 'she is wanted to make things the way Jesus would want her to do.

Mother I am going to lay down; I am tired I have a big day tomorrow all at once there was a knock at the door is this where the girl we saw preaching today lives? yes who are you her mother asked?

Tammy came to her mother the man said; wait here I have something for you; he came back with loads of things; they put the things on the porch; here is things we all gather for your family; and we brought everybody somethings that lives in the Neighborhood;

her dad came out of the room thank you so much; you are so welcome; we really like your preaching; and we felt sorry for the familys here; knowing what you said; about everyone was poor; we wanted to help out the others are happy; God answer your pray little girl; they were praying to; Mr yes I am sure they were .now we brought clothes for you mother and dad;and you; and food I know; you will feel better the furniture is coming in we got your mother a new table; you said something; about your mother and the old table she seat at; here is your mother a new table; look mother for you; a bed and couch chairs; thank you Jesus said Tammy; after the people left the family were looking at what they got; her dad was so happy' he put his arms around his family; he told his daughter he wanted her to lead him in a sinner pray; ok dad; are you sure? you want be doing the things you did before. Yes kitten I do I know God is real look at all the things we got; this change my mind ok dad she lead her dad in a sinner pray he had tears; in his eyes; she know he had given his heart to God' the mother and daughter the little Muskteer Tammy were all Gods children; they begain to look at all the things the news people had given to them; look mother a new dress just my size; yes dear here is one for you mother; and Dad a pair of pants; Towels wash cloth lots of things; night dress shoes and food now we can have more than bread; yes dear the days are passing by they have what other people have now; one day there phone ring Tammy pick it up; who is it dear mother I have someone on the line wants me to preach; at there church in Janurary; they said they would call back next year; ok dear; they said they would pay for my trip; if I would preach at they Church; we will talk later we have only 3 days till christma I am going to our playhouse my friends are waiting on me. Are you going to eat before you go? mother I have eaten so much I am good for while; I need to go see them she left; when she was walking to see her friends; they came where she was so happy; in new clothes eating just looking diffrent; than before thank her for having faith in God; she was telling them what she got; they all said what they have; they all were so happy new clothes new shoes Furniture food telephone ice box lots of things; the whole street was diffrent; Tammy told her group about the call she got; they were happy for her she was still preaching for her little Musketeer; many people had been saved under her minstery she could not stop now; lets all seat on our new Furniture the Lord gave us; the seats were all fell up; its time to start my preaching; first of all I wont to thank God for all he has given to us here on 18 street; we are not poor anymore; I wont to welcome you all to my minstery you can feel at home; we were all in this Neigsborhood so blessed since I have been on live tv we have people everywhere giving us things we are so thankful; it is only 3 days to Christmas we have recived so much God is good; now I want to lead anyone to Jesus; make your way up here; I love you all lets love Jesus; there was over 100 people assept Jesus tammy saw so many camers there in diffrent state they all come up to talk to her; she was so happy; before the Revival was over; she was talking to so many people; why she did preached to anyone; who would listen; she told them it was Jesus that was who she wanted people to know; now she is home her mother has got the house looking so pretty; she heard a knock at the door; its the people on her street; come on in her mother said they wanted to see Tammy; we all come down to thank your daughter; for praying for us all never have we saw anyone with such faith; we did not believe it would happen when our children told us' we made fun of it Tammy we come here to say we are sorry; you made a believe out of us; we have got so much now we are blessed; its ok I know some people would not Believe it; everyone cannot be on the same line; some of them will fall off; thank you all for stoping by; our kids they Believe in you; so what we have got to say keep on leading our children the right way; it is amazing what you have done; in our Neighborhood thanks; they hug Tammy and left; mother I am over joyed to see what God has done for all our people it has made a change in our life; I am so happy to know people beleive; in miracle; there is no stopping us not; the girls are so happy; since

God answer our prays; mother I will go lay down now; a knock at the door her mother answer; it was the men from the neighborhood; we wont to see your husband; Bill some men are here to see you; tell them to come in; my husband will be out soon; out comes her husband; we come to let you know we got a job today start to work monday; did they called you;? let me asked my wife honey did anyone call me about a job? let me see she reached in her pocket had a peace of paper; here is something; let me see yes it has a number for me to call; we have all got a job monday; another pray answer said one of the men we have been to church praying about a job; now we have one; well it is time to go home we are all so happy since your little girl prayed for all of us; we are so blessed see you later; they left mother I am going to bed now; I like that new bed in my room and the bed clothes it is so nice; every thing is nice; she told her mother and Dad goodnight; and went to her room we still need more toyes for the ones on 18 street; now Amen; she walked over to the window looked at the sky all of Gods; creation 'now it was time to go to bed; the next morning' she ran to the kitchen her mother was making breakfast; Mother that bacon sure smell good seat down I will make you some eggs; I have got to hurry the group are waiting on me; you can take a little time to eat; mother it fees so good to know we are not poor anymore; we owed it all to God you see mother God does answer prays; yes I know that; my Dad is a christian now we all love Jesus' now I am ready to go to do God work' your mother and me will give you support 'thank you Dad; I will go now it is time for all to gather at my mistory; as she was walking to the playhouse; she saw many people making there way to her place of pray 'she got a supprise; they had made the place where her playhouse was in a bulding; The Church of God Tammy and little Musketeer she thank God as she walk in side; she saw her friends on the front rool in the room behind her was her playhouse with lots of toys the girls lead her to them; after she got there lots of people from all over the world come to her Revival; and to her left was the news people; in front were news from diffrent states; she was so happy when they all seat down she wanted to welcome them all; after the service she had some people to asked her questions; she looked around some of the ones she lead to the Lord was there; she had so many people they were out side looking in; she had lead 1000 to Jesus her speach was Jesus and many miracle they were listen to what she said the Bible she had; was given to her by her grandma; she let them know about things her grandma had told her to serve the Lord; it was time to go back home the next day was Christmas; God had work many miracle in her and friends lives; when she was back home; the phone ring her mother answer; it was from some people that was giving away a car in a drawing; they wanted to meet at her Church; her mother told her; she said mother not in side we will bring the chairs out side; her Dad call all the men to meet him at the Church; her mother accept the offer; her Dad and the others got things ready; they met at the out side of her Church; the drewing began; the first was 18 they got all the numbers in the box' everyone draw a number Tammy was by her Dad; did you draw Dad? yes now one of the ones giving the car away; draw the number the number her Dad had was 18 you won Dad I see someone coming foward here is the one that gets this car; what is your name Bill Johnson mr Johnson Congratulations you are the owner of a 61 ford fairline we are happy to give it to you' taxes free; here are your keys everyone MR Johnson is the father of the one who owns this bulding we are seeing the younger preacher we have know; we have four more to give away Mr Johnson is driving his car away with the papers; when they got home it was geting late; her mother made supper 'they had chicken mash potoes gravy good for a king; after supper Tammy asked her mother to help put some giffs together for her friends they did and they carried them to there house; they gave Tammy some giffs for her familly it was going to be the best Christmas every; it was time to go to bed; Christmas tomorrow; goodnight mother and Dad they both said goodnight; when Tammy was in her room' she feel down on her knees; dear Jesus thank you for every thing; you have made us the best Christmas ever my little friends are so happy; now I do not beleive in santa but it is christmas time so could you send us a angel in a red suit that is what we see down here; you dear Jesus are the reason for the christmas day; thank Lord for sending souls to be saved; Amen.

Tammy went to the window as she did everynight saw God creations; we to sleep the next morning she heard her Dad and mother in the kitchen; she went to them;what is going on mother; we have so many presents here and one is for your Birthday; open it kitten her Dad said she begain pulling off the paper in front of her was a Certificate with her name Tammy Sue Johnson the youngest paster to preach with a 500 dollars for her Birthday; she was so happy to fianly get what she has been working for; something was going out side she and her parents step out side; to see santa in a red suit; thank you lord every thing was so good; she had the people standing at her door to wish her merry Christmas; I give it all to Jesus please all my little Musketeer come stand by me this is where it all begain we lived in a poor house; we all pray to Jesus to change everything; now instead of a poor house we all have Jesus to thank it happen before Christmas; I have a Certificate for me to preach; tell everone about Jesus merry Christmas everybody may you have a blessed year coming.

The End

www.ingramcontent.com/pod-product-compliance
Lightning Source LLC
Chambersburg PA
CBHW030141100526
44592CB00011B/991